Fats, Oils, and Sweets

Ann Thomas

CHELSEA
CLUBHOUSE

An Imprint of Chelsea House Publishers
A Haights Cross Communications Company
Philadelphia

Chelsea Clubhouse
1974 Sproul Road, Suite 400
Broomall, PA 19008-0914

The Chelsea House world wide web address is www.chelseahouse.com

Library of Congress Cataloging-in-Publication Data

Thomas, Ann, 1953-
    Fats, oils, and sweets / by Ann Thomas.
    p. cm. — (Food)

    Includes index.
    Summary: Presents information on the fats, oils, and sweets group of the USDA Food Guide Pyramid, describing some of the foods in this group, their uses, how they are processed, and their role in nutrition.

    ISBN 0-7910-6979-6
    1. Oils and fats—Juvenile literature. 2. Confectionery—Juvenile literature.
    3. Nutrition— Juvenile literature. [1. Oils and fats. 2. Sugar. 3. Confectionery. 4. Nutrition.]
    I. Title. II. Food (Philadelphia, Pa.)
    TX560.F3 T46 2003
    613.2'84—dc21

                                                                                    2002000026

First published in 1998 by
MACMILLAN EDUCATION AUSTRALIA PTY LTD
627 Chapel Street, South Yarra, Australia, 3141

Copyright © Ann Thomas 1998
Copyright in photographs © individual photographers as credited

Text design by Polar Design
Cover design by Linda Forss
Illustrations © Anthony Pike

Printed in China

Acknowledgements

Cover: Great Southern Stock

Australian Picture Library/J. P. & E. S. Baker, p. 14; John Shaw/Auscape/Coo-ee Picture Library, pp. 10, 15, 20; Great Southern Stock, pp. 4, 8, 13; HORIZON International, pp. 18, 27; Getty Images, pp. 12, 17, 28, D. V. Matthews/ANT Photo Library, p. 23; The Photo Library-Sydney, pp. 6 Jenny Mills, 9 ©Sheila Terry/SPL, 11, 16 ©Robin Smith, 19 ©A.G.E. FOTOSTOCK, 21 ©CC Studio/SPL, 22 ©A.G.E. FOTOSTOCK, 26 ©Chris Everard, 29 ©Chris Everard; Stock Photos/Wally Hampton, p. 5; U.S. Department of Agriculture (USDA), p. 7.

While every care has been taken to trace and acknowledge copyright, the publisher tenders their apologies for any accidental infringement where copyright has proved untraceable.

Contents

Why Do We Need Food?

We need food to keep us healthy. All living things need food and water to survive.

We also eat foods because they taste good.

Elephants eat bushes and other plants.

There are many kinds of food to eat.
People, animals, and plants need different
types of food.

What Do We Need to Eat?

Foods can be put into groups. Some groups give us **vitamins** or **minerals**. Some groups give us **proteins** or **carbohydrates**. We need these **nutrients** to keep us healthy.

We need to eat a variety of foods.

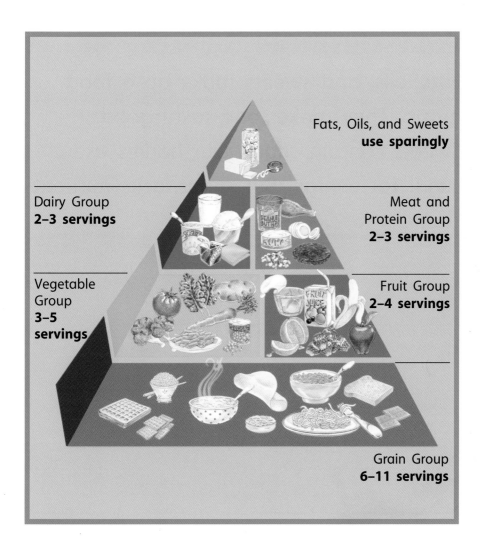

The food guide pyramid shows us the food groups. We should eat the least from groups at the top. We should eat the most from groups at the bottom.

Fats, Oils, and Sweets

Fats, oils, and sweets make up a food group. They make food taste good. Sweets contain sugar. Our bodies use sugar for energy. But sugar lacks nutrients.

There are many kinds of sugar.

Some oils come from olives or sunflowers. Butter is a common fat.

Fats and oils provide energy, too. Our bodies can store the energy as body fat and use it later. Fats and oils also help us take in vitamins and minerals from other foods.

Our bodies need only small amounts of fats, oils, and sweets. Eating too much sugar can cause tooth **decay**.

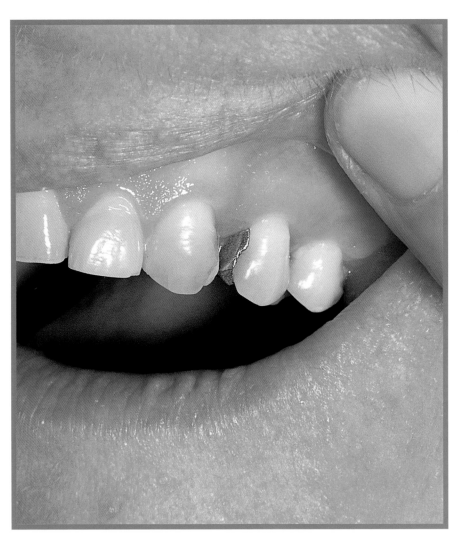

Teeth need fillings when sugars cause decay.

Maple syrup has a lot of sugar. Butter and bacon have a lot of fat.

Eating too many fats, oils, and sweets can make us overweight. A diet high in fats and oils can also damage the liver. The liver cleans extra fat from our bodies.

Where Do They Come From?

Fats, oils, and sweets are found in natural products. They can also be **manufactured**. Sugar comes from **refining** the juice in sugar cane and sugar beet plants.

The juice inside this sugar cane stalk will be refined to make sugar.

Butter is a fat that is sometimes used to cook vegetables.

butter

Fats and oils come from meat, milk, and some plants. Both fats and oils are used in cooking. Fats are solid and oils are liquid.

Making Sugar

Sugar cane grows in warm, tropical places such as Hawaii. The cane grass grows between 10 and 26 feet (3 and 8 meters) tall.

These are young sugar cane plants.

This machine cuts up the long stalks of sugar cane.

Machines **harvest** the stalks. At a factory, other machines crush the cane's tough **fiber**. This leaves a juice. The juice is boiled, filtered, and refined into raw sugar crystals.

Workers rinse the raw sugar crystals. They dissolve the crystals in water again and pour the liquid through filters. Then the liquid is heated. White sugar crystals form.

Sugar is made at refineries.

Eating too much sugar can cause health problems.

There are higher levels of sugar in our diets today. As a result, more people are developing health problems. Sugar-rich diets can lead to one kind of adult **diabetes**.

Making Olive Oil

Olive oil comes from olives. Workers pick ripe olives. Then large machines crush them and press out the oil. The oil is collected.

An olive tree produces many olives.

Factories crush olives several times to make different grades of oil. The process is called cold pressing. Finally, workers boil the crushed olives to remove the last drops of oil. But it is a poor quality oil. The oils are bottled for sale.

Other Fats and Oils

Oils can come from many plants, such as sunflowers. Meat from animals can also be boiled to remove oil.

Sunflower oil is often used for cooking.

Margarine is soft and spreads easily.

Margarine comes from whipping
vegetable oils or animal fats. Margarine
can be substituted for butter. Butter is
a fat made from milk.

Natural Sugars

Most foods have natural sugars. Fruit and honey are rich in natural sugars.

Honey ants store honey in their bodies.

Honey bees and honey ants make honey.
They eat sugary liquids made by certain
plants and turn it into honey. Many
flowers have sugar in their petals. They
also create a liquid called nectar.

Honey is used to sweeten many foods. Baklava is a very sweet and sticky Middle Eastern pastry. It is made with honey.

Baklava is made with pastry, nuts, and honey.

Maple trees make a sweet liquid called sap.

Some trees make sugar. Maple tree sap gives us maple sugar and maple syrup.

Sweet Foods

Sugar makes food taste sweet.

Candies and chocolate contain a lot of sugar.

Fatty Foods

Meat eaters have more fat in their diets than **vegetarians**. Fat is naturally found in meat. Hamburgers contain fat from beef cattle.

French fries are very high in fat.

Fats give some foods extra flavor. Fried
foods contain a lot of fat.

The Fats, Oils, and Sweets Group

These foods have natural fats and oils.

avocado

cheese

cashews

These foods have natural sugars.

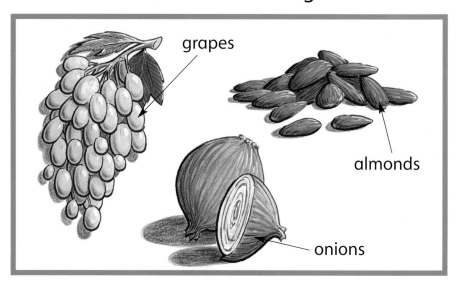

grapes

almonds

onions

Glossary

carbohydrate   an element found in certain foods that gives us energy when eaten; bananas, corn, potatoes, rice, and bread are high in carbohydrates.

decay   to rot or break down

diabetes   a disease where people have too much sugar in their blood

fiber   the tough inner portion of a plant

harvest   to gather in a crop

manufacture   to make a product, usually in a factory

mineral   an element from earth that is found in certain foods; iron and calcium are minerals; we need small amounts of some minerals to stay healthy.

nutrient   an element in food that living things need to stay healthy; proteins, minerals, and vitamins are nutrients.

protein   an element found in certain foods that gives us energy when eaten; eggs, meat, cheese, and milk are high in protein.

refine   to make pure; a refinery is a factory that purifies a substance.

vegetarian   a person who does not eat meat

vitamin   an element found in certain foods; Vitamin C is found in oranges and other foods; we need to eat foods with vitamins to stay healthy.

Index